Book 2

Sure-fire Phonics

Ann Williams and Jim Rogerson

Nelson

Thomas Nelson and Sons Ltd
Nelson House   Mayfield Road
Walton-on-Thames   Surrey
KT12 5PL   UK

51 York Place
Edinburgh
EH1 3JD   UK

Thomas Nelson (Hong Kong) Ltd
Toppan Building 10/F
22A Westlands Road
Quarry Bay   Hong Kong

Thomas Nelson Australia
102 Dodds Street
South Melbourne
Vic 3205   Australia

Nelson Canada
1120 Birchmount Road
Scarborough   Ontario
M1K 5G4   Canada

© Ann Williams and Jim Rogerson 1980
Illustrated by Oxford Illustrators Ltd

First published by E J Arnold and Son Ltd 1980

This edition published by Thomas Nelson and Sons Ltd 1992
ISBN 0-17-410243-7
NPN 9 8 7 6 5 4

Printed in Hong Kong

Contents

Look at the pictures. Say the words.

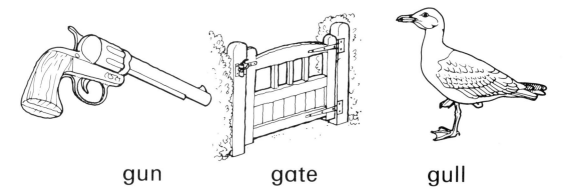

gun   gate   gull

Read these letters. Write them in your exercise book.

1. g   g   G   G
2. G   G   g   g
3. g   G   b   B

Read these words. Write them in your exercise book.

1. gag   2. gas   3. get   4. gill   5. got   6. gull

7. gum   8. gun   9. gut   10. bag   11. beg   12. big

13. bog   14. bug   15. cog   16. egg   17. fig   18. fog

19. leg   20. log   21. Meg   22. mug   23. nag   24. peg

25. pig   26. sag   27. tag   28. tug

Choose one of the words in each box to complete the sentence.
Write the sentence in your exercise book.

1. log leg	2. gum gun
A gull is on a _____.	It is a _____.
3. beg egg	4. mug tug
It is a big _____.	The _____ is on the mat.
5. leg beg	6. peg pig
Pat's _____ is cut.	The _____ is fat.

Look at the pictures. Say the words.

dog   duck   doll

Read these letters. Write them in your exercise book.

1. **d**   **d**   **D**   **D**

2. **D**   **D**   **d**   **d**

3. **d**   **D**   **g**   **G**

Read these words. Write them in your exercise book.

1. Dad	2. Dan	3. deck	4. den	5. Dick	6. did
7. dig	8. dim	9. din	10. dip	11. dock	12. dog
13. doll	14. Don	15. dot	16. duck	17. dug	18. dull
19. bad	20. bed	21. bid	22. bud	23. cod	24. fed
25. god	26. kid	27. lad	28. led	29. lid	30. mad
31. mud	32. nod	33. pad	34. pod	35. sad	36. Ted

Choose one of the words in each box to complete the sentence.
Write the sentence in your exercise book.

1. dull   doll

The _____ is in the mud.

2. bed   bad

Dad is in _____.

3. dig   big

Ted can _____.

4. dot   dog

The ___ sits on the sack.

5. duck   deck

It is a big _____.

6. nod   cod

The gull picks up the ___.

Read these words. Write them in your exercise book.

| and | and | and | and |

Read these sentences. Write them in your exercise book.

1. Bill and Ben sit on the tub.

2. Mum and Dad met Don.

3. Sid and Mick sell pens.

4. Ann and Pam fill the tins.

5. Tim and Mick dig in the mud.

6. The dog and the pup sat on the mat.

7. Sam and Ann met Mum on the dock.

8. Tom and Pip pack the bags.

9. Ken and Sam toss Tom's cap.

10. Bob and Tim dig up the moss.

Look at the pictures. Say the words.

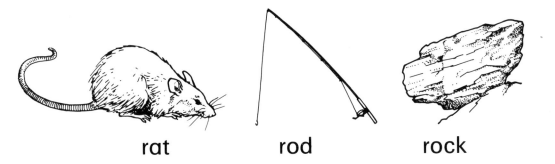

rat   rod   rock

Read these letters. Write them in your exercise book.

1.   r   r   R   R
2.   R   R   r   r
3.   r   R   d   D

Read these words. Write them in your exercise book.

1. rack   2. rag   3. ram   4. ran   5. rat

6. red   7. rib   8. rid   9. rig   10. rim

11. rip   12. rob   13. rock   14. rod   15. Ron

16. rot   17. rub   18. rug   19. rum   20. run

21. rut

Choose one of the words in each box to complete the sentence.
Write the sentence in your exercise book.

1.   ribs   rips

The pup _____ the bag.

2.   ram   rag

It is a _____ doll.

3.   rock   rack

It is a big _____ .

4.   run   rug

The pup sits on the _____ .

5.   rot   rat

The _____ got the egg.

6.   rod   rob

Tom's _____ is on the rock.

Look at the pictures. Say the words.

hat   hen   hut

Read these letters. Write them in your exercise book.

1. **h**   **h**   **H**   **H**
2. **H**   **H**   **h**   **h**
3. **h**   **H**   **r**   **R**

Read these words. Write them in your exercise book.

1. hack	2. had	3. hag	4. ham	5. hat
6. hem	7. hen	8. hid	9. hill	10. him
11. hip	12. hiss	13. hit	14. hod	15. hog
16. hop	17. hot	18. hub	19. hug	20. huff
21. hull	22. hum	23. hut		

Choose one of the words in each box to complete the sentence.
Write the sentence in your exercise book.

1.   hot   hat

Mum has a big _____ .

2.   hut   hug

The _____ is on the hill.

3.   hen   hem

The _____ has ten eggs.

4.   hum   ham

It is a _____ .

5.   hips   hops

Sam _____ on the mat.

6.   hill   hid

The bus is on the _____ .

Look at the pictures. Say the words.

| jam | jug | jet |

Read these letters. Write them in your exercise book.

1.   j   j   J   J
2.   J   J   j   j
3.   j   J   h   H

Read these words. Write them in your exercise book.

1. jab   2. Jack   3. jam   4. jet   5. jib

6. jig   7. Jill   8. Jim   9. job   10. Jock

11. jog   12. jot   13. jug   14. jut

Choose one of the words in each box to complete the sentence.
Write the sentence in your exercise book.

1. jam   jab

The _____ is in the pot.

2. jig   jug

The _____ fell on the rug.

3. Jill   jet

The _____ is big.

4. Jack   jog

_____ and Jill
run up the hill.

5. Jock   job

_____ digs in the mud.

6. Jim   Jill

_____ sits on the rock.

Look at the pictures. Say the words.

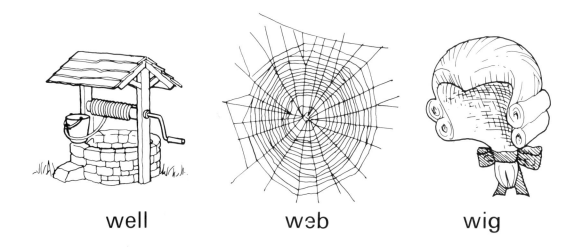

| well | web | wig |

Read these letters. Write them in your exercise book.

1. w   w   W   W
2. W   W   w   w
3. w   W   j   J

Read these words. Write them in your exercise book.

1. wag   2. web   3. wed   4. well   5. wet

6. wick   7. wig   8. will   9. win

Find the words in the bag with **w** in them.
Read these words. Write them in your exercise book.

1. _____   2. _____   3. _____   4. _____

5. _____   6. _____   7. _____   8. _____

9. _____

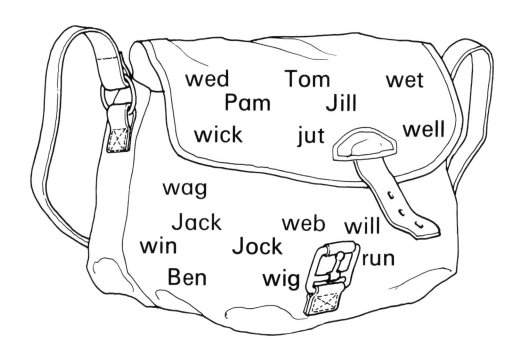

wed   Tom   wet
Pam   Jill
wick   jut   well

wag
Jack   web will
win   Jock   run
Ben   wig

Read the sentences. Choose the right words.
Write the sentences in your exercise book.

1. The cat fell in the (will, well).

2. It is a big (web, wed).

3. Ben will (win, wick).

4. Pat has a (wig, will).

5. The dog is (wed, wet).

Look at the pictures. Say the words.

yak   yacht   yawn

Read these letters. Write them in your exercise book.

1.   y   y   Y   Y
2.   Y   Y   y   y
3.   y   Y   w   W

Read these words. Write them in your exercise book.

1. yak   2. yam   3. yap   4. yell

5. yen   6. yes   7. yet

Find the words in the bag with **y** in them.
Read these words. Write them in your exercise book.

1. _____   2. _____   3. _____   4. _____

5. _____   6. _____   7. _____

yam   wag
yap   yak   it
wig   Jim   yet
will   yes   hen
yen   yell   dog
wick   lid

Read the sentences. Choose the right words.
Write the sentences in your exercise book.

1. The pup (yaps, yams).

2. (Yet, Yes), Jim is in the bus.

3. Bill (yells, yes) at Bob.

4. Is the jug full (yet, yes)?

Look at the pictures. Say the words.

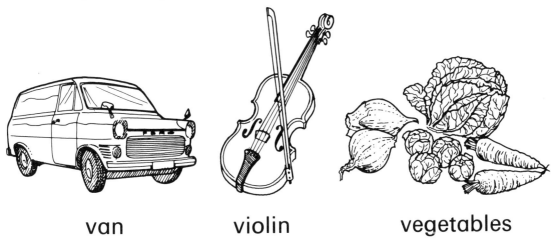

van   violin   vegetables

Read these letters. Write them in your exercise book.

1. v   v   V   V
2. V   V   v   v
3. v   V   y   Y

Read these words. Write them in your exercise book.

1. Val   2. van   3. vat   4. vet

Find the words in the bag with **v** in them.
Read these words. Write them in your exercise book.

1. _____ 2. _____ 3. _____ 4. _____

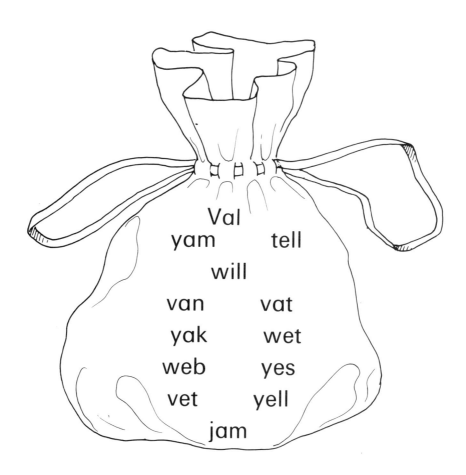

Val
yam   tell
will
van   vat
yak   wet
web   yes
vet   yell
jam

Read the sentences. Choose the right words.
Write the sentences in your exercise book.

1. It is a big red (van, vet).

2. (Val, Vat) has a doll.

3. Ron is a (vat, vet).

Choose one of the words in each box to complete the sentence.
Write the sentence in your exercise book.

1. wed   web

It is a _____ .

2. wig   win

Mum has a _____ .

3. van   Val

It is a big _____ .

4. vat   vet

Dad is a _____ .

5. will   well

The cat sits on the _____ .

6. yells   yet

The man _____ at the dog.

Look at the pictures. Say the words.

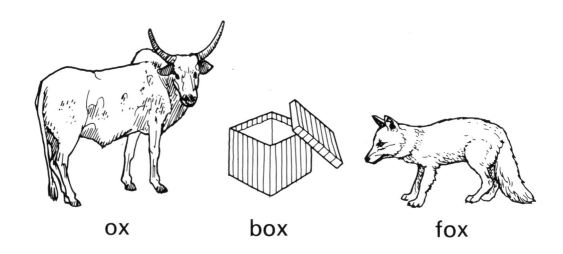

ox   box   fox

Read these letters. Write them in your exercise book.

1.   x   x   **X**   **X**
2.   **X**   **X**   x   x
3.   x   **X**   v   **V**

Read these words. Write them in your exercise book.

1. tax   2. wax   3. vex   4. fix   5. mix

6. six   7. ox   8. box   9. cox   10. fox

Find the words in the bag with **x** in them.
Read these words. Write them in your exercise book.

1. _____   2. _____   3. _____   4. _____

5. _____   6. _____   7. _____   8. _____

9. _____   10. _____

ox

vat   six

box   Val   vex

yell   fox   tax   vet

cox   web   wax   ill

fix   van   mix

till

Read the sentences. Choose the right words.
Write the sentences in your exercise book.

1. I can sit on a (box, mix).

2. Pat has a (tax, wax) doll.

3. The dog has (six, fix) pups.

4. The (cox, fox) is in his den.

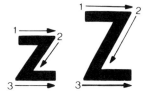

Look at the pictures. Say the words.

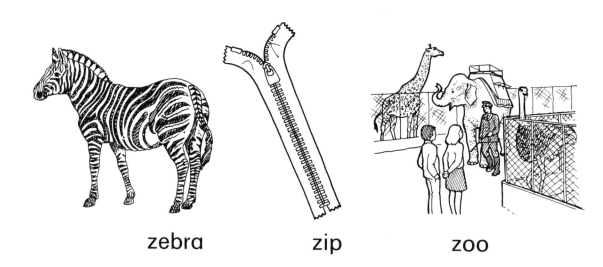

zebra   zip   zoo

Read these letters. Write them in your exercise book.

1.   z   z   Z   Z
2.   Z   Z   z   z
3.   z   Z   x   X

Read these words. Write them in your exercise book.

1. zigzag   2. zip   3. buzz
4. fizz   5. fuzz   6. jazz

Find the words in the bag with **z** in them.
Read these words. Write them in your exercise book.

1. _____   2. _____   3. _____   4. _____

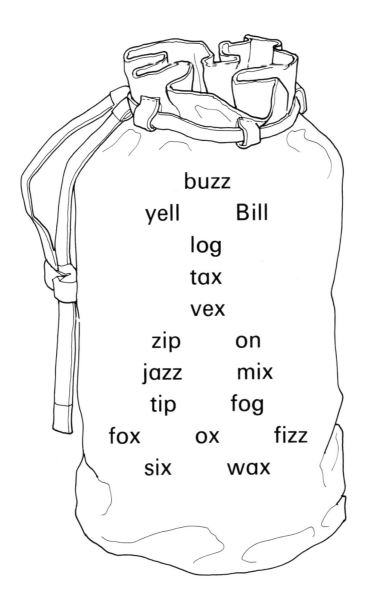

buzz

yell   Bill

log

tax

vex

zip   on

jazz   mix

tip   fog

fox   ox   fizz

six   wax

Choose one of the words in each box to complete the sentence.
Write the sentence in your exercise book.

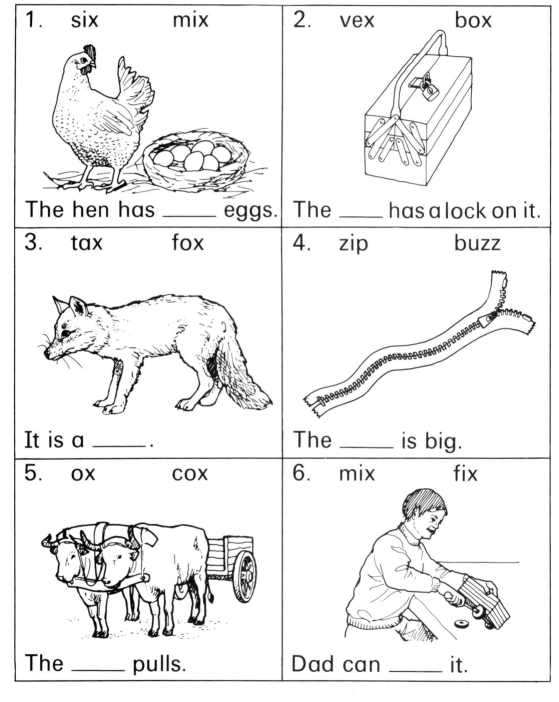

1. six mix	2. vex box
The hen has ____ eggs.	The ____ has a lock on it.
3. tax fox	4. zip buzz
It is a ____ .	The ____ is big.
5. ox cox	6. mix fix
The ____ pulls.	Dad can ____ it.

Look at the pictures. Say the words.

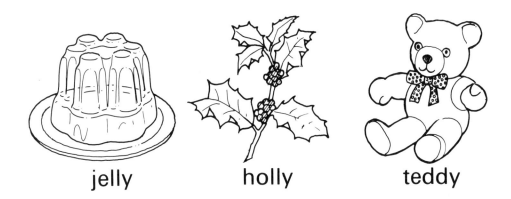

jelly   holly   teddy

Read these words. Write them in your exercise book.

1. Daddy   2. Danny   3. rally   4. Sally

5. jelly   6. Jenny   7. Kenny   8. teddy

9. Billy   10. hilly   11. silly   12. Bobby

13. hobby   14. lobby   15. holly   16. jolly

17. Molly   18. Polly   19. Tommy   20. dummy

21. Mummy   22. tummy   23. funny   24. sunny

25. fussy

Choose the right word from each box to complete the sentence.
Write the sentence in your exercise book.

1. Jenny   jelly

It is a _____.

2. sunny   funny

It is _____.

3. teddy   Tommy

Sam has a _____.

4. jolly   holly

The _____ is in the pot.

5. lobby   Daddy

_____ has a rod.

6. Sally   silly

_____ fell in the mud.

Draw these crosswords in your exercise book.

Across

1.

2.

4.

5.

6.

7.

9.

Down

1.

3.

5.

7.

8.

Now you can read these words:

a	bit	cup	egg	gas
am	Bob	cut		get
an	Bobby		fan	gill
and	bog	Dad	fat	god
Ann	boss	Daddy	fed	got
at	box	Dan	fell	gull
	buck	Danny	fen	gum
back	bud	deck	fib	gun
bad	bug	den	fig	gut
bag	bun	Dick	fill	
ban	bus	did	fin	hack
bat	but	dig	fit	had
bed	buzz	dim	fix	hag
beg		din	fizz	ham
bell	cab	dip	fog	hat
Ben	can	dock	fox	hem
bet	cap	dog	full	hen
bib	cat	doll	fun	hid
bid	cock	Don	funny	hill
biff	cod	dot	fuss	hilly
big	cog	duck	fussy	him
Bill	cot	dug	fuzz	hip
Billy	cox	dull		hiss
bin	cuff	dummy	gag	hit

Now you can read these words:

hobby	jazz	lad	men	nip
hod	jelly	lap	mess	nit
hog	Jenny	lass	met	nod
holly	jet	led	Mick	not
hop	jib	leg	mill	nun
hot	jig	less	miss	nut
hub	Jill	let	mix	
huff	Jim	lick	mob	off
hug	job	lid	mock	on
hull	Jock	lip	Molly	ox
hum	jog	lit	mop	
hut	jolly	lobby	moss	pack
	jot	lock	mud	pad
	jug	log	muff	pal
I	jut	loss	mug	Pam
if		lot	Mum	pan
ill		luck	Mummy	pat
in	Ken			peck
inn	Kenny			peg
is	kick	mad	nag	peg
it	kid	man	nap	pen
	kill	map	neck	pet
jab	kiss	mass	net	pick
Jack	kit	mat	nib	pig
jam		Meg	nil	pill

29

Now you can read these words:

Pip	rock	sip	tip	wick
pin	rod	sit	Tom	wig
pit	Ron	six	Tommy	will
pod	rot	sob	top	win
Polly	rub	sock	toss	
pot	rug	suck	tub	yak
pub	rum	sum	tuck	yam
puff	run	sun	tug	yap
pull	rut	sunny	tummy	yell
pup				yen
	sack	tack	up	yes
rack	sad	tag		yet
rag	sag	tan	Val	
rally	Sally	tap	van	zigzag
ram	Sam	tax	vat	zip
ran	sap	Ted	vet	
rat	sat	teddy	vex	
red	sell	tell		
rib	set	ten	wag	
rid	sick	the	wax	
rig	Sid	tick	web	
rim	sill	till	wed	
rip	silly	Tim	well	
rob	sin	tin	wet	